Biscuits for Bunter

A Dog's Diary

. . .

Biscuits for Bunter

A Dog's Diary

written for him
by
Helen Merriman Fernald

FOURPAWS PRESS
Cambridge, Massachusetts

. . .

Biscuits for Bunter
A Dog's Diary
by Helen Merriman Fernald

Published by Fourpaws Press
18 Reservoir St., Cambridge, MA 02138

Book design, typography & electronic pagination by
Arrow Graphics, Inc., Watertown, Massachusetts
Printed in Hong Kong

Library of Congress Card Catalog Number: 97-090402

ISBN: 0-9658181-4-4

. . .

To Syd,
who encouraged the book's publication,
and Alvart and Barbara,
who helped to accomplish it.

· · ·

CONTENTS

. . .

Puppy Kindergarten ... 1

CAMBRIDGE

Early Days ... 5
Cat Time ... 8
Money ... 11
Sick Days ... 13
Fight Night ... 15
Meal Time ... 18
Holiday Problems ... 20
Bad Things ... 23
Food Mischief ... 25
Exploring ... 29

MAINE

Cruising and Other Terrors ... 35
Island Life ... 43
Love Life ... 47
Love, Lobsters, and Fog ... 50
Bones and Bird Seed ... 54
Smelly Days ... 58

FINAL DAYS

Autumn Days, Cooler Days ... 63
Later ... 66
Not Good Times ... 69

Epilogue ... 71

. . .

Puppy Kindergarten

I've just finished eight hours of Puppy Kindergarten and I've got a big piece of paper to prove it. It says right there, in capital letters, that Bunter Fernald has completed the Pre-Novice Course.

Don't you think I deserve a biscuit as a graduation present—even though I knew how to sit, stand, stay, and lie down long before Missus took me to class. I've been doing these things naturally all my life, though of course not at someone else's command.

Pre-Novice is about as low as you can get, but I think that is all Missus is going to do with me because she says I am hopeless and only want to play. Well, I can't help it if my tail never stops wagging. The teacher says Missus is hopeless and will never train me properly because she is giving me unconditional love instead of love on the condition I obey her. Not so. There were at least thirty dogs of all sizes and shapes barking and yelping all the time, so no one could hear the commands anyway. Furthermore, the teacher told the owners that they must train their dogs to adapt to their life-style. Well, that should be a two-way street. Luckily I've fallen in with people who like the same things I do—good friends, good food, a warm bed, comfortable chairs and sofas.

I made a major decision recently. Since I'm so observant of people behavior, now that I have my diploma, I'm going to keep a diary of my thoughts and their activities.

Cambridge

. . .

Early Days

My first few months don't count much. I only remember a crisp fall day, full of life and excitement, when some people came to meet me at the kennel. I was introduced to a Mr. and Mrs. but I couldn't remember their names, so I have always called them my M and Missus. I jumped, wiggled and ran in circles and worked my way into their hearts. Love at first sight. They were going to take my sister, too, and name us Simon and Schuster, long before they knew I was going to be a famous author, but Missus said one cocker was enough, and she picked me and called me Bunter.

After some talk with the kennel man about diet, shots, worms, and money, we got into a car. My first trip was not so pleasant, as we whizzed along. I felt queasy and drooled onto a towel, but I didn't get sick. After a while we came to a driveway and she said, "Welcome home." I didn't know what a home was, exactly, but after running about the garden and all around the inside of the house, I decided to stay with them forever.

Now I am learning about daily routine and chores. It starts with getting off their bed in the morning, which is a slow process. I've learned to let sleeping humans lie. Later I help sort out the garbage, picking over any items that are still edible. Humans are wasteful. I am an avid vacuum cleaner when it comes to crumbs of toast and bacon on the floor, but I can't reach the counters yet—and Missus isn't about to lift me up.

Almost every day a person comes to the front door with lots of pieces of paper. Apparently this person is a male-man. What a dumb thing to call him. Of course he is. If he was a woman would he be called a male-woman, or a mail-female? I'm not supposed to bark at him. M sorts out the envelopes and fusses at some of them called bills, then takes me for a walk to get the newspaper. His life seems to be dominated by paper. Walking is something else. How can I run with that string attached to me? He says he is eating too much and has to walk it off. Well, the more I walk, the more I want to eat. Humans are inconsistent.

If there is time, we play. I don't understand this game. There is a box filled with old rubber balls, and M picks one out, stands in the middle of the garden, and throws it away. I like to chase the balls, so I go and fetch it for him. Then he throws it away again—and again—and again. If he has collected them all these years, why does he insist on throwing them away? I get exhausted running back and forth. He stops to pat me and says, "Good dog," which I appreciate, because I know I am, and I'm happy to please him. But really, this is stupid. Then Missus comes out and takes her turn, throwing the ball so high into the blue sky that it lands in the neighbor's garden, where I can't reach it.

Even the police do dumb things. They sent notices to everyone about poops, warning that people would be fined $10 for the first offense, $15 for the second, and $25 for the third if the owners did not pick up after their pooches. This is totally silly. How can they know whose pooch pooped where, and whether it is the first, last, or always offense? They can't possibly carry out this threat. So we continue our habits, along with everyone else, though M and M carry "mutt-mitts" for pickups.

I know an elderly lady who walks her dog in the city park every morning at seven o'clock sharp—not six or eight—because she wants her dog to associate with the "better breeds of upper-class dogs," whatever that means, which take their morning walk at that hour. This same lady told us about her friend who took an old purse, lined it with plastic, and went about the city streets in the late evening, picking up what had been left behind, to help keep the sidewalks clean. But one dark night a nasty jogger came along and snatched her purse. Though she was terrified, she must have had a good laugh thinking about the surprise he was in for when he opened it up. Serves him right.

Cat Time

I've got a real problem. There is a cat here, smaller than I am, and I'm having difficulty coping with her. She is light brown with chocolate ears and tail and very blue eyes, which is all right as far as cats go, I guess. (But they don't go very far—or not far enough for me.) Her name is Kitnip, which doesn't suit her at all, so I refer to her as just plain Cat. Apparently she just arrived one night, when she was very small, uninvited, as a stray, with no I.D. tags or papers saying she'd had shots. M and M took her in, gave her food and shelter, and tried to find out where she belonged, but there was no interest, of course, so they ended up keeping her, sneezes included. They fixed their sneezes with pills and they "fixed" her too.

I have a lot to put up with, such as scratches to my nose and eyes and being jumped on from a chair as I walk by. I am trying to be friendly and even share my bed with her. But she takes up the biggest half, and pushes me away with stretched-out legs. "Ask not what your cat can do for you. Ask what more you can do for your cat than give her your food and bed." Everybody knows that quote!

M and M have some really big plants growing in the bay window. I admit to peeing on them occasionally, especially if Missus has forgotten to water them. Of course, I get caught and punished. The odor can ruin the lovely smell of gardenias. But one time Cat did it. Missus actually saw her. I was delighted, and couldn't wait for the scolding. But it never happened. How come? I don't think that is fair.

I hear there is a lot of stuff going around about Fairness and Equality for Women, so I suppose Missus is practicing this new fad on Cat. But then I heard her talking about an article she had read by a famous vet, who wrote that if a

cat messes outside her litter, the cat is trying to tell you something. Maybe she doesn't like the brand of litter, or maybe she's sick.

Cat never said anything to me. She just let fly. Missus took this accident very seriously and did not punish her at all. Instead, she took her to the vet—which might be considered a punishment by some.

Sure enough, Cat did have a problem, and she had to stay in the hospital for several days. But I'm not going to go into her problems because I'm writing about mine. Anyway, it was made clear to me that one does not spank cats. It just isn't done.

On the plus side, Cat is good company when we are left alone, and we curl up together. But she does get special privileges and has even been known to walk on the type-writer and piano keys. Missus thinks this is funny. Some joke!

An old man called Mark Twain said, "If you find a starv-ing dog, feed and care for it, and it prospers, it will never bite you. That is the fundamental difference between man and dog." I have another version, which goes like this: "If you find a stray cat, bring it into your house, and care for

it, it will take over almost everything you have, from chairs, sofas, beds and blankets to food. This is the fundamental difference between me and Cat."

Money

I don't understand why people get so riled up about money. They fuss about it—whether to spend it or save it. All I care about is having enough to buy my food. And maybe some left over for Cat.

Missus exploded when she read an advertisement for petsitting at $5 an hour. That comes to $120 a day. If M and M go away for ten days, forget it! Twelve hundred dollars just for the privilege of watching me? Of course, on second thought, it is a privilege for them, so, on third thought, it is I who should be paid, since I give so much pleasure and comfort to others. Perhaps this money thing needs rethinking.

Missus says that her children only get $5 an hour for watching other people's babies, and that includes cooking, feeding, diapers, and other messy things. Am I to understand that pets are more valuable than children? Hmmmm.

M read an article about a man in New York who hires a limo once a month just to take his dog to a beauty parlor downtown to get his fur washed and cut. I don't get that kind of treatment. I get washed in the laundry tub in the basement, then clipped on a bench outside, so my fur blows away and won't mess up the house. It's sensible and inexpensive.

M read about a camp for dogs sort of like Outward Bound for people. For $800 for two weeks, a dog goes through all sorts of horrors to make him tough, obedient, and self-confident. Nonsense. I am as obedient as I choose to be, certainly think well of myself, and I didn't go to camp.

Now M and M have gone and bought a new car. It is a dead ringer for the old one, only ice blue instead of filthy silver, and it smells new. The old one had over 100,000 miles on it; anyone would have some problems if they had run that far. They got the last model on the lot and were told they'd saved a bundle. How can they spend so much and still save a pile?

The first time I jumped in, I immediately saw an ideal spot for Cat to sleep. Right above the dashboard is a great place to curl up in the sun, with a view through the windshield of what is coming up next; I think it was meant for coffee mugs, dark glasses, Kleenex, and last week's mail. But I know who is going to use it. She will love it and it isn't big enough for me.

The ads for this car show a whole family with five kids, a deflated rubber swimming pool, luggage, toys, a picnic basket, and equipment of all varieties being squeezed into this van. But these pictures do not include a dog or even a lesser animal, like Cat. There simply isn't room for them, what with all the kids and junk. If cars cost so much, they should have room for dogs. Lee "Iaccoconut" definitely needs to get this message and redesign his cars to include dog-space.

Sick Days

I don't feel well. No, not at all. Sometimes, without warning, I start to shiver and shake all over. My legs get stiff and I can't quite stand up. I wake up on the floor, and Missus is holding me tenderly, wiping my eyes and mouth, speaking gently to me. "It's all right, Bunter."

M and M took me to the hospital. A kind vet stuck pins in me to get blood and took pictures of my tummy while people held me motionless. He said I was the most trusting dog he had ever known and I was a "lamp chop" to handle. Then he said I had a severe sickness, and I might never get better. I must take pills every day of my life or something terrible could happen. I love my family so much and I have a lot of living to do, so I will try to swallow what he says.

While we were waiting for the results of the tests, I saw and heard some awful things. There is a place in that building where Owners can leave their dogs and cats, if they don't want them anymore. Some get put to sleep forever. I don't understand. Why did these Owners get pets in the first place if they didn't want them for life? How can you throw away a person? I suppose some of the more lucky and healthy ones could get chosen to live with someone else, but the mere thought that they could be thrown away is pretty horrible. People take advantage of the fact that we can't speak; we can't even choose with whom we want to live, or tell them when we feel sick, cold or hungry. I wondered how it would be if nobody cared for these Owners and disposed of them? Still, they can talk, and tell their story. We depend on understanding, mercy and compassion. I began to realize that not all people care as much as mine do ... except those Vet-People, who care for me and all my friends.

I saw a rolling stretcher-bed go by with a big dog on it. His leg and paw were mashed and mangled from being caught in an escalator. I hope his Owner didn't throw him away just because he couldn't walk.

I was glad to get home that afternoon. I was even glad to see Cat. I have decided to get on with my life and put all these miseries out of my mind.

Fight Night

One evening M took me out for our usual walk. I was snuffling about in the bushes and leaves, looking for a place to relieve myself, when a scruffy dog came around the corner and attacked me. My neighbor's dog was barking at him and maybe he got nervous, but he was a real hyena at heart, with no manners. The next thing I knew I was in the middle of a commotion, with shouting and yelling, growling, and other disagreeable noises. Ugly business. He was trying to bite me. It isn't my nature to bite, because it isn't a very subtle thing to do, but this time I thought I'd return the favor. The dog's Owner was trying to intervene. So was M. There were a lot of legs to choose from, and maybe I chose the wrong leg, but suddenly the Owner got very angry. After some more scrapping, M got me leashed and pulled me away. That gave the man a chance to get his dog tied up, too.

Then the two men started to argue about the leash law and who was at fault. Well, they both were, but M was less so, since we were still close to our driveway, and he hadn't had time to leash me yet. The Owner lived a mile away, so he'd had plenty of opportunity.

Never mind. I thought we should part company and let the matter drop, since no one was really hurt. I just knew inside that there was going to be real trouble later.

When we got home, M told Missus what had happened. She gave us Holy Hell. She stated that if I'd been properly leashed and on the other side of the street, none of this would have occurred. She said that the man might come and sue us, since M had pointed out where we live. From the way they were talking, I thought I might have to be sent away. I didn't sleep well for a few nights, worrying this over and over. I don't think Missus did either.

Sure enough, early Sunday evening the doorbell rang. Who should be there but that man, without his dog. He said he was scared to come in for fear I'd bite him. I put on my best friendly act, rolling over, shaking paws, and wagging my tail until he was utterly disarmed and smiling. But he was being oily and much too polite as he oozed his way through the door. There appeared to be something more on his mind than me. There was.

Money.

There we all were in the front hall. Actually, Missus was rocking back and forth from one leg to the other, so I knew she was nervous. Her expression told me that she smelled a big, fat rat underneath the chit-chat going on between the men.

Suddenly the man took his pants down, right there in front of us, to show us a tiny blue bruise on his upper thigh. He claimed I'd made it. He began talking about needing medical attention, doctor's bills and shots—and he didn't mean whiskey. He said he needed a hundred dollars to get checked out at the clinic.

M stopped smiling and stiffened up some. He replied in a measured voice, "Nonsense, it is only a small bruise and no blood was drawn. How do you know Bunter did it, anyway?" The man said it was painful, which was not the answer to that question. I went into the library and got up on the chair for comfort as I thought I didn't have much to add.

After more discussion, I heard Missus say we would give him twenty dollars for an appointment at the clinic, but that was all. I don't know why she gave in. It seemed to me she was admitting some guilt, which was not right. I guess she wanted to get over the whole episode quickly, so I didn't blame her. On the whole, giving in was cheaper than rabies tests and vet bills for me.

The owner became oily-friendly again and said "Goodbye and thanks, Perfesser." He was wrong on that count too.

After he left, M said, "Bunter, you're a damned expensive dog." I don't what he meant. Expense is not the issue. Besides, he knows I am priceless and invaluable and he loves me to pieces.

Mealtime

It is Sunday, a glorious fall day, and I have had a good time. That is, until midafternoon.

I was outside with M and M while they raked leaves. It was fun, jumping into the pile of leaves they had made and scattering them about so they had to do it all over again. Two hours of joyous foraging. But at three forty-five I knew that it was almost time for dinner. I have a built-in clock. It's accurate, too. M and M are always aware of time. I've trained them well.

I quit playing, cocked my head to one side, and stared at Missus with that "I am hungry" look. It clearly said that it was quarter to four, which is when I eat.

She stopped raking and looked at me and then at her wristwatch. "No, Bunter, it is only quarter to three." She resumed raking.

I informed her, by jumping on her, that her stupid watch must have stopped or was broken and to look again. She did and said, "It is only *two* forty-five."

How did that *two* get in there? Things were going from bad to worse. Anyone can tell you that going backward in hours is not good, especially where food is concerned. The word I like best is FOOD; and the next best words are MORE and NOW.

She tried to explain. "It is always like this once a year, Bunter. It is the end of Daylight Saving Time." As if my tummy cared about that. "I'll tell you what we'll do. We can split the one-hour difference if you can wait for thirty minutes for your supper today and again tomorrow, then everything will be back to normal." Waiting is *not* normal for me, and I didn't really understand. But I played about some more and finally got my supper at three-fifteen her time, four-fifteen mine.

Well, I had a good chuckle when it got to be six o'clock my time, though only five hers. She was pretty tired from raking and was thirsty for her "usual," which they have at six. She said to M, "Hey, don't you think it's about That Time? I'm weary." He looked at his watch and then raised his eyes to meet hers. "Well, it's really only five o'clock. Don't you think we should wait until six?"

There was dead silence, followed by frowns and sour expressions. Then more wristwatch checking. I was looking at her, and she knew it.

Then in a muted voice she murmured, "Oh, all right. I suppose, maybe, … er … how about starting at five-thirty just for tonight?"

That was a great ending to the day. It just goes to show, two legs or four, we have a lot in common.

I wonder what happens to that hour of light and why they save it? Where do they put it? In the fridge? The light goes on and off in there. All I really want is that hour back; and I want my supper on time—not an hour late.

Holiday Problems

It is getting close to Christmas, and I am anxious. M and M went in town to do something at a place they call K.C. I am not sure where it is or what K.C. stands for. Kennel Club? Kitnip and Cats? Keep Clean? Kibbles and Chunks? (I like that one best.)

When they came home they said they were going to wrap some presents. I hope they don't forget me. When they do all that wrapping, I hang around because I like to tear up the bits of paper that fall on the floor. It also keeps me busy—a good arrangement. But last year was nearly a disaster. I chewed up their list of people who were going to get presents, and Missus was not pleased. Was my name on that list, and had my present been done up already? (I don't know about Cat's present, or if her name was even on the list. She doesn't know about Christmas, so why not keep it that way.)

The second thing that worries me concerns trees. M and M bring in a small green tree which they set up in my favorite window, where I sit and watch the squirrels eat up all the bird seed in the feeder. I use trees outdoors to relieve myself, so I thought I could save myself a trip in the cold and wet and use this indoor one. Apparently it isn't done. I was scolded and told not to do it again. But I forget when I'm in a hurry. Humans forget too—especially things they don't want to remember. After all, it's a whole year between Christmases. One year for people is seven for me, so how can I possibly remember what happened eighty-four months ago?

Holidays get me sort of stirred up. Halloween is bad enough, with all those kids coming to our house to get goodies. I don't get anything, and I'm told not to bark at them. Next year I think I'll dress up as a big, bad bear. Thanksgiving is something else. I've never seen such a hullabaloo over a dead turkey. Last November I met a young dog whose people had come for the big feast. His name was Dinsmore. I don't know what kind he was—a new breed, an old breed, or no breed at all—but he was awfully big and tall. He came inside and immediately put his nose in the eggnog punch, which was on the coffee table, just to try it.

When Missus put the bird in the oven, we were both sent outside to play. Everyone stood around while we had a fine romp, sniffing, running, and jumping. Dinsmore was sort of clumsy, and when he fell off the garden wall, his owners said, "Uh-oh. Dinsmore's potted!" I tried mounting him, but he wouldn't stand still. Everyone was laughing at my efforts, giving me encouragement, such as "Nice try, Bunter, but the wrong end." I don't understand. Isn't one end as good as another?

While all this was happening, Missus forgot the turkey and it got overcooked. Too bad. It was one tough hen, anyway. (Cat got some lickies, but I think she threw up later.)

Now I'm concerned about the kitchen. It's just too small—long and narrow like a Pullman car. I like to be there most of the time because that's where the action is. It really is the best place in the house.

The problem is that M and M take up too much room. They were very thoughtful, though, and put down two foam rubber mats, one in front of the sink and the other in front of the stove. This is perfect placing, showing a full understanding of my needs. The one next to the stove is my favorite because sometimes goodies drop down, and the smells are overpoweringly scrumptious.

Of course I lie on them all the time—that is what they're for. But sometimes Missus's feet are there, too, and if I am there first, she has to straddle me. M's feet are even bigger. I know my teacher said we had to learn to adjust to our people's habits, but I think they should also adjust to ours once in a while, and this is a *once* they are not doing. Missus speaks rather rudely to me: "Move it." This does not happen to Cat, because she sees Missus coming and simply gets up and moves off to sit in front of the hot-air vent, thereby blocking my warmth. I just can't win. Furthermore, when Megan, a golden retriever, visits us, efficiency goes out the window. That makes sixteen legs and feet. Too much.

Bad Things

Some bad things have been happening—and not all of them were my fault, either. The cellar got flooded from too much rain and melted snow, and the washing machine overflowed. I was afraid M and M were going to blame me for all that water, but fifty Bunters could not have accomplished that lake, not even five hundred cats. While they were mopping up, I was put outside because my soaking paws made squishy marks on the rugs, which added to the mess. Eau de Wet Water wafted through the whole house.

I think all this was the weatherman's fault. I heard him say on the radio that it was going to be warm and sunny. That was four days ago. Talk about bad forecasting! It poured cats and cats, all over my fur coat. He did say there might be scattered showers, so I fulfilled that prophecy, at least, by shaking off in the front hall.

Another thing that happened maybe was my fault. M and M had arranged to have the house painted, as it had not been done for years and looked pretty shabby. The painter came in his truck, and before he even started to paint, he "loved me up" quite a lot and told me I reminded him of his own puppy. I like that kind of person.

He was too busy to play with me for long, so when he parked his truck in the driveway and left the door open, I jumped in to investigate. All the paint cans were sealed, but I did smell something yummy. After snuffling about for a while, I found his luncheon sandwich on the dashboard, east to reach. So I ate it, wax paper and all. It was very good, despite the mustard. The painter caught me with a mouthful as I jumped down from the truck. But he didn't seem to mind very much, especially when Missus said she would make him another one.

I was wondering how I could get that one, too, and in my haste to get to the kitchen, I pushed the front door open with my nose, where the painter had just finished with his white brush. As a result, I got white paint all over one side of my head. This was not very smart. When Missus saw me, she knew exactly what had happened. She lifted me up on the counter, got the scissors and Oster-shaver, and went to work on my head. Now I look all lop-sided: one side soft and curly, the other just about naked. And I got hiccups from the wax paper.

Food Mischief

Life is a bit flat now that the holidays are over, and I am suffering from terminal boredom. It has been a dull week here in Cambridge, but we do have two bright red cardinals, which add some color to an otherwise drab, unkempt, woody, weedy garden. These redbirds outdo Cardinal Law by a long shot. The squirrels are everywhere, fat and saucy, eating up the spilled bird seed. When I chase them, my nose is glued to the ground, so I often go headlong into the tree trunk while they go straight up. My vet told Missus that I have two detached retinas in my eyes from bashing my head. This makes it hard for me to see, especially at night. Well, I can't see these retinas, so this doesn't stop me during the day. The ground is frozen and the running is swift.

Being cooped up inside is different, and not having enough to do often leads to trouble. I just made another wrong mistake when I ate a chunk of M's fur hat—the front part, which shows the most. There it was, sitting on the front hall chair. Irresistible. Missus fussed at him for leaving it there. Too tempting, she said. So it wasn't really my fault.

They left me in the kitchen when they went out, as a sort of punishment. It's somewhat confining and has no decent chairs. I was miffed until I found something to do. Missus keeps raw vegetables in a bin: potatoes, onions, and other good things to eat. I found a potato that clearly said,

"Eat me." It was hard, and yellow inside. I ate it. It passed the time nicely. Later I didn't feel so well.

Missus didn't notice anything when she returned, and I certainly didn't tell her; but the next day she wondered why, when I relieved myself in the bushes, things were yellowish. That evening she decided to have baked yams for supper; there was only one left. She didn't say anything but grinned at me. She knows everything.

I'm in the doghouse again today because I ate M and M's luncheon spiced beef. Nice and fresh, it lay on the edge of the table, wafting an enticing smell. Of course I jumped up quickly, got the whole half pound, and ran straight outside to eat it on the grass. What a delicious picnic! But I got punished and spoken to very severely.

I think M and M understand how boring it is to be left in the house alone for too long. Quite often they take me to the city with them, even to Meetings, where they know I am acceptable. Most of the people there know me quite well, and I actually get a lot of attention. They sit around a big table and talk and talk and talk. I fall asleep; what they say is totally boring—they don't even mention food. One time a man came in late, spied me under the table, and, interrupting everyone and pointing at me, said in a loud voice, "*What* is that *dog* doing here?" I thought I'd have to leave and be put in the cold car to wait for hours. But a friend spoke up on my behalf in an even louder voice. "That is *not* a dog. *That* is *Bunter*." That fixed his wagon. He sat down and I stayed put.

Recently, we've had fires in the house—the nice kind in

the fireplace, I mean. A friend gave us some of those kerosene-saturated briquettes that get the flames going but look like macaroons. M bit into one, thinking it was a biscuit. He chewed it a little and spat it out because it tasted so awful. Missus rolled over laughing, but he didn't think it was funny at all. I started to chew on one of the twig kind, but she took it away because she thought I might get splinters in my mouth.

I've heard that word *splinter* before. One afternoon, M and M spent a long time fixing goodies for some friends to munch on—thin slices of ham with cream cheese, rolled up and fastened with a toothpick. They left these tidbits on the coffee table while they went to greet people at the front door. I thought I'd sample one or two, just to be sure they were tasty. Missus had a fit, not only because of the loss of her goodies, but also because she thought I might have swallowed some of the toothpicks, which would stick in my stomach. They didn't.

One has to be careful what you eat around humans. I heard Missus talk about the big poodle who swallowed her opal ring. She had taken it off because it was big and clumsy and got in the way of her typing, so she put it on the low table beside her machine. The poodle came along and gobbled it up, spitting out the setting but swallowing the opal. She tracked that dog everywhere when it went out, which was quite often. It was a messy affair. Luckily, it had been snowing for several days, so the garden was clean and white. Two days later her search was rewarded. She retrieved the opal and had it reset. She was told that it is considered bad luck to wear opals unless your birthday is in October. Hers is in January.

That summer, a spider bit Missus's finger when she was asleep one night. When she woke up, her finger was all swollen and purple, and she couldn't remove the ring. She had to go to the jeweler, who sawed it off. The ring, I mean. That time she did not have it reset. She sold it.

Humans do strange things. I think I'd best stick to my own food and not experiment with theirs. Last night they had dead chicken, green ferns, stale rice, and cookies for dessert. Kibbles and meat for me, please.

Exploring

M and M are talking about going away somewhere. I'm curious and hope it includes me (and I suppose Cat). I've not been many places outside our home, and I wonder if there is more to Massachusetts than our garden. I try to wander around a bit, but I usually can't get past the chain-link gate.

I was able to take advantage of the heating man's carelessness the other day. When he came to fix the furnace, he left the gate open, so I could ooze my way out to investigate, broaden my horizons, and become worldly.

I set off at a gentle trot, sniffing hydrants, shuffling around the leaves, mully-grubbing in the bushes, and lifting my leg where I chose. I do know the territory pretty well from all my walks, though I have never done it on my own. The freedom was great. I even crossed some streets, and a car screeched its brakes at me, but I got out of the way in a hurry. I saw a cat pussy-footing down an alley, but it didn't look like Cat, so I left it alone. There were some trash cans on the sidewalks, but they were empty. Other dogs, taking their people for walks, passed me and wagged their tails, but they didn't have time to stop and sniff. I met one enormous dog, as big as a pony; I got stiff and tense, prepared to attack, defend, play, or fade away quickly if necessary. But he didn't even acknowledge me. He ignored me completely. Not even a tail wag. I was quite insulted. Am I that insignificant? I may be small, but that's no reason to be rude.

I was beginning to think about supper and where I might find it—if at all—when a car pulled up beside me and stopped. A big man got out, came toward me holding out his hand and said, "Come here. Let's get in the car." This sounded like a nice offer. I thought he might even give me some supper. It never occurred to me that I might be dognapped.

I got in his car, and he smiled at me as we drove along. Pretty soon I began to recognize my own neighborhood. What did he do but turn down our driveway, tooting his horn as he pulled up to the front door! I was astounded, though a bit disappointed that my adventure might be coming to a grinding halt. When he rang the doorbell Missus appeared, looking rather distraught. She seemed to know him, and she thanked him very much for returning

me. Then she lit into me for leaving the yard. The heating man had left, so he wasn't there to take the blame for leaving the gate open. Missus had noticed that I wasn't around the house, and she had been looking for me up and down the streets, thinking she should call the police about a missing dog. She told me I was very lucky that a friend had recognized me. I could have been hit by a car or had one of my seizures and been put in a garbage can. I stood there, looking sheepish. I realized that it was her love for me that made her so angry. I decided then that I wouldn't go on any more expeditions. So much for my ambitions—and her realities.

I remembered the time Missus and I were driving through the city. We saw two men in a car with the top down, radio blaring, open the car door and push out a lovely black labrador who had recently had puppies. Missus pulled up beside them at the red light and asked if that was their dog and what were they doing? They snarled back at her, "We don' wan' her no more. Mind your own fuckin' business." They took off at top speed through the traffic. We looked everywhere for that dog, but she had disappeared in the tangle of cars, and we couldn't find her. I've never seen Missus so angry or upset. She stopped the car on a side street to get control of herself, then leaned over and hugged me. I agreed. It was awful. We wondered where the dog's pups were. Probably thrown into a Dumpster to die.

Another time, when we went to Harvard Square early one very cold morning, we noticed a man tie his German Shepherd to a lamppost and walk to the subway with a suitcase. We had to go back to the Square late in the afternoon, and the dog was still there, shivering, waiting patiently for a thoughtless Owner who never intended to return.

Missus loves dogs so much that I think she would take in all the lonely, hungry, lost, and rejected dogs she could find if there was room. I wonder what would happen to me, smothered by so many. M says, "Not to worry, Bunter. It won't happen." But I heard her talking on the phone to somebody at a kennel, where there were ten puppies. She said she didn't even dare go to see them for fear she would come home with nine. And they weren't even strays! M said, "Fat chance." Actually, she finally said, "Good-bye," and hung up the phone. A narrow escape.

Maine

. . .

Cruising, and Other Terrors

I am somewhere else. It is called Maine. We left Cambridge and drove for five long hours to get here; I am tired from car lag. M and M packed the car-van so full of food, jackets, and baggage that there was no room for me except on the floor between them, where it was stuffy. Cat got the best place, of course, on the dashboard in the sun; when it got too hot she moved back to the jackets, in the shade.

While we drove along, I heard on the radio that there are supposed to be 330 breeds of cats and five million more cats than dogs in this country. I don't know how big New England is, let alone the whole country, but whoever did the counting never asked us if we had a cat. They could be off by several hundred thousand with such sloppy behavior.

We almost lost one of them—ours—recently. It was a harrowing experience.

A few days after we got settled in our island home, M and M decided to take Cat and me on a four-day cruise and visit some friends. This was fine with me. I didn't consult Cat, as she would not have had a valid opinion.

The four of us set off on a glorious morning, though it was a trifle windy and rough. Cat went below and threw up and then went to sleep. Missus had to clean up the mess. I didn't get sick but snoozed on the cabin floor, waiting to get somewhere I could plant my paws firmly on land. It was a long wait. Things kept sliding about on the boat, falling off bunks and counters onto the floor, so good sleep was impossible. M and M had lunch as they went along, but I didn't get any, and Cat still slept. They kept oohing and aahing at the pink granite boulders and cliffs on the shores they passed, but they never once stopped to take me for a walk on them.

When they got to the Eggemoggin Reach (or Wretch, as Cat would have called it), everything got flat and calm, and Cat woke up. Missus straightened things out below, and I came up to see why we were slowing down. Soon M reached the mooring he wanted, which was convenient— for me, that is, because he could row me ashore, at last, to do my business. Which we did, and I had a good romp, too. Cat stayed on the boat. She didn't seem to mind, since she had her own litter under M's bunk. Handy. She got her exercise walking around and around the deck of the boat, morning and evening; and she got her amusement sitting on the edge of the stern in the evening, watching the gulls swoop down, looking for some crumbs from dinner. I sort of wished she would make a pass at one of them and fall in. I doubted that she was as good a swimmer as I am, so that might be interpreted as a death wish—which, in retrospect, was not very nice.

We all slept well that night, and Cat recovered from her seasickness quickly. The next day dawned rainy, miserably wet and choppy. I got my business trip ashore taken care of promptly while Missus did up the breakfast dishes.

When we returned I heard her ask, "Where is Kitnip? I don't see her anywhere." "Oh," said M, "She must be  around here somewhere. You can't get lost on a thirty-four-foot boat." Are you kidding! They looked everywhere: No Cat. Missus was frantic. "She could have gone out for her morning walk, slipped and fallen in. We might not have heard the splash with all the sloshing noises. Oh, please get in the dinghy again and go look for her." M got the long fishnet pole, just in case he could find her swimming, or worse, her floating body in all that icy water. Missus kept looking through the binocs, but the rain and her teary eyes didn't help much. There wasn't much I could do except stay out of the way, sit, and wonder. I began thinking how much I really loved Cat, how much I would miss her, how much I had maligned her, and other awful thoughts and worries. She was my best companion, my foil, my friend.

I'd have no one to blame for my mistakes, no one to cuddle with, no matter whose bed we were on.

So we waited and waited, while M rowed and rowed in larger and larger circles, finding nothing. Missus was calling: "Kits, Kits, Kits." Eventually he came back. In despair they made another complete boat search. Nothing. No one. No Cat—no Kitnip. Missus left the cabin and went out to the cockpit to call once more, with a terrible urgency in her voice. And then, in a lull of waves and weather, she heard a very faint "Meow-ow-ow." Where did it come from? She called again, hoping for another answer, and indeed there was another faint "Meow-ow-ow." It sounded as if it came from under the floorboards, down in the bilge. How did she ever get there, and even more puzzling, how were we to get her out? I was worried—and was

very glad it wasn't me. Little did I know that my own turn of terror was coming up soon.

M and M ended up by lifting the floorboards, one by one, and there she was—one wet, scared, miserable cat. If we had started the engine, I guess she could have been made into mincemeat, or cat-meat—a gruesome thought.

They lifted her tenderly out of the bilge and set her down on the cabin floor to see what she would do. Sure enough, she went straight to the small hole she had gone through—a hole no bigger than a grapefruit, which had once held a pipe, running the length of the boat. This hole was in the back of a small cabinet under a bunk, and they had never noticed it. M and M sealed it off with some stuffing very quickly once Cat showed it to us. And that was the end of that!

Cat looked at me as if to say: "Well, it is completely natural for me to explore every inch down here, especially when the weather is too rough and wet for my morning walk. But you know perfectly well that I am so surefooted that I would *never* slip and fall in! Ridiculous! However, I was curious, and since one place led to another, I kept on going. How was I to know that it dead-ended in such a foul place? Now I have to clean off all that oily water I got into. What a mess!" She had rather a haughty vocabulary, which complemented her creamy chocolate fur coat, blue eyes, and stylish demeanor. I just listened and wagged my tail. I was so very glad to see her, and she knew it. So much for curiosity almost killing our cat.

M and M had another cup of coffee and we set off for our next mooring. As the day went by, the sun came out, though the wind didn't let up much. I was bit unsteady on my legs. Cat didn't throw up again, even after doing her lick-wash job on her coat. She settled into her blanket to sleep.

About four that afternoon, getting near my suppertime, we finally got to Fox Island Thorofare, where M's friends lived. At last I was going to be able to run around some-

one's grass and not have to go on cold, wet rocks and slimy seaweed. M and M found the right mooring. M slowed down and headed into the wind, which by then was very strong. Missus went forward with another long pole, with a hook on the end of it to catch the mooring. I thought I would follow her, to supervise this operation and give her support, even though my ears were blowing backward like Piglet's, streaming in the wind. The mooring was bobbing up and down and the boat was wallowing in the waves, so I knew it was going to be tricky. Missus saw me coming and called out very firmly, "No, Bunter. Go back." I did stop, at least, but it was at the most narrow place of the entire deck and there was no turning-around space. Dogs very seldom walk backward, and neither do I.

I'm not sure whether it was a big wave that threw me off balance or if I misjudged the few inches I had, but I fell overboard—a five-foot drop into the coldest water I'd ever been in. Terrifying. I surfaced, but with all that salt water in my eyes, which stung, I couldn't see, and all that water gurgling in my ears, I couldn't hear. Instinctively I knew how to paddle just to stay on top, but I didn't know where to go. The tide was going out fast and the current was taking me with it. Missus's voice, calling me, got fainter and fainter, and the waves pushed me about like a cork. I couldn't paddle against these mountains, so I was losing ground—or water—rapidly, getting farther and farther away from the boat. I could hardly keep my head up to breathe.

Missus saw what was happening. She dropped the pole and went back to the stern, got into the dinghy as fast as she could, and rowed after me. M stayed at the wheel, turning the boat so I wouldn't get tangled up in the suction of the engines, but by that time I was so far away and so tired and cold, I just wanted to give up and go to sleep, sinking down, down into a bottomless hollow.

Then I felt a firm hand on my collar, a strong arm under my chest, and Missus pulled me up, dripping wet, into the dinghy. I shook off all that cold water, and she held me tight in her arms, hugging me. We were both exhausted. She thought I was a "goner"—whatever that is, was, or might have been.

We rowed back to the boat, which by this time was a long way from the mooring, having drifted in the wind and tide. But who cared, now that I was safe. First things first! I got toweled off and went below to the warm cabin while Missus went forward to get the mooring once again. Cat slept through the entire affair. Really. M and M changed their clothes and we three took off for the shore. We left Cat some dinner in case she woke up, but closed the cabin door so she wouldn't go exploring anymore.

Land, oh blessed land! I know some big dogs who love to swim, but their fur coats are thicker than mine, and they are much stronger and used to the water. I am a land dog—a house dog—preferably a warm house dog. And we went to one, where a nice lady greeted me and said I could lie by her fire or use her lawn if I needed to. I did both. Some of the people we visited had big dogs, and when I told them my story, they looked bored. Oh, well....

I learned a lot from that cruise, and one can moralize all one wants about the change in my attitude toward Cat. Never mind. What's important is that we all survived. And we were all very glad to get home once again.

Island Life

I'm getting used to life on this island, and I love it. There are no streets, no trucks, no banging trash cans or noisy sirens—but also no stores. This could pose a problem, as I want to be sure we can buy food for my supper. But I saw M and M lugging lots of packages, bags of food and boxes of stuff, up the hill to our house, and so I assume there is something for me.

I can run free wherever I want. Missus is afraid I will get lost in the forest and keeps calling me, just to be sure I know my way home. I do.

Strange, there are no squirrels here at all; at least, I haven't seen any. Maybe they all left for Cambridge. There are big white birds, which squawk at one another and at me, but I can't chase them as I am stuck to the ground. And I have seen my first deer. They are very queer, with sticks coming out of their heads and long, spindly legs. They like to eat Missus's flowers, which she just spent a lot of time planting in her garden. I run and chase them away, but they never tell me which way they are going, and speed doesn't help if you are going in the wrong direction.

Every other day we go to town to do errands in the little run-about boat. I don't know why they call it a run-about, because boats don't run exactly, and ours is no exception. Sometimes it doesn't run at all. Often I'm allowed to go with them. Cat always stays home.

Town is great. I see lots of people who love me to pieces and give me compliments. One of the best places is the Post Office, where I get lifted up on the counter and the mail-ladies rub my ears, scratch my head-bone, look deep into my eyes, and love me up considerably. Another best place is the store near by, where I get a biscuit, while Missus tries on beautiful clothes. That's nice.

The last trip we made turned out to be pretty iffy. We had done a lot of shopping and really overloaded the boat with boxes and packages, so we had very little free-board and were floating low when we left the harbor. The wind was puffing up some, and the waves were sort of swampy, so we went along slowly and carefully, bobbing up and down. I didn't feel too well, and I didn't want to get soaking with the spray, so I lay down at Missus's feet and hoped we would get home soon.

Suddenly we stopped, and I heard M and M shouting to somebody, so I got up on the seat to see what was going on. There was a man in a small power boat trying to row it, because the motor had failed. He waved to us for help, though we were hardly in a position to do much. But you can't just pass by as if you didn't notice. So we got the towing line, and after throwing it several times, he finally caught it and made it fast. We started off again, towing him very slowly because of all that weight and the rough seas. Our little engine was chugging along but sort of gasping. M looked at the gas gauge; it read Empty. Oh, great! I had visions of us all drifting out to sea. I was sure we would never get home for supper.

We slowed down a bit and called to the man that we didn't have enough gas to take him to his island first and we could only make it to our dock. Of course, he had to go along with us. However, he was very friendly, and he helped us unload our boat and carry all those packages up the hill to our house, which is an enormous haul. We offered him a cool drink and the use of our telephone.

Then M remembered the three-gallon tank of fuel he had stored in the shed for emergencies. I went with him to help supervise while he poured the gas into the boat. Missus and I watched them take off for the man's island and said to "come again any time!" I am not sure what we meant. Missus thought it was terribly kind of M to go to all that trouble, but he said that since the man had helped us to lug the stuff up the hill, it was only a "quid pro quo"—whatever that is.

What really burned me up was that once we got all those boxes into the house, piled by the front door, Cat knocked over the thermos. She was glad to see us, I realized, but she didn't need to be so bouncy. Naturally, I got blamed. On top of that, Cat got up on a high chair, and when I walked by, she swiped me with her paw. Ambushed from above—I could do without that annoyance. After all, I had had a rough day myself, and she didn't need to treat me like an animal.

Love Life

I have just met the MOST dog anyone could imagine, and I think I am in love. Her People are friends of M and M's, and when they came to the island for lunch the other day, they brought her along.

Her name is Jasmine—"Jazz" for short, which suites her, because she is. Short, I mean. Her legs are not as long as mine. That is good, because I can outrun her. She is part Pekingese and part Lhasa-Apso-Ipso-Facto or something. I don't care which part is which; I just love her all over.

When she jumped out of her boat onto the float, I was right there to greet her. M and M were helping tie up the boat, but we were free to run. We streaked up the long pier into the tall grass, tearing through the lupine, racing through the ferns, tumbling and rolling over and over with hilarious joy. We got so tired we had to stop and lie down, panting and smiling at each other. It was love at first sight. Her fur is long and tawny; her eyes are pools of midnight brown. Her tail hooks up over her back and joins the rest of her fur, falling to the ground, sweeping the grass. She is just gorgeous. I only hope she thinks I am handsome as I dash through the bushes, like black lightning.

We humped back and front, rolled and chased all afternoon, until it was time for her People to go. Missus suggested to them that Jazz and I get together and have puppies. (I think, the way she said it, she meant Jazz to have them—not me. I don't know how. I've never done this kind of thing.)

I thought that mixing it up with Jazz could produce a whole new breed, which I'm sure would be very popular. I've heard of all the different breeds of dogs at the Westminster Dog Show, in New York, so I know there's no breed like ours would be. I was also thinking in terms of millions ... not puppies, but dollars.

But my dreams faded when I heard the People say that Jazz had been "fixed." (I thought they only did that to cats. Thank heaven it hasn't been done to me.) Missus said, "Oh dear! Too bad."

After Jazz left, I began feeling very lonesome and sad. I curled up on the sofa, thinking about the wonderful time we'd had and hoping that even if we couldn't have puppies we could still get together to play. I was missing her very much, so I wrote her a poem, my first.

Jasmine, oh Jasmine! Where are you, or has been?
Oh, Holy Cow! Where are you now?
And who will care, if I am HERE, and you are THERE?
Except me.

So much for doggerel. I can't think of anything to rhyme with that last line. Maybe it's better that way. I'm more in the mode of whimsy than vast erudition. Get it right the first time, and leave it alone. (I know people who have a Ph.D. in Boredom, talk a blue streak, and never get anything right.)

Love, Lobsters, and Fog

I saw Jazz again the other day when we went to town. We played on her front lawn and had a great time; she acted as if she still loved me. I certainly think she is wonderful. Her People invited me inside their house, which was rather spiffy and elegant, so I had to be on my best—at least better—behavior. Jazz was very provocative and tantalizing. She got up on her bench by the fire and just lay there, looking at me and panting. Since it was a single bench, there was no room for me. I suggested to her that she might have a double bench, so I could snooze with her. When we left, I gave her a final snuffle, and hoped I would see her again.

Going back to the island was strange. We went into a new kind of weather called fog. They say that it "comes in on little cat feet." I've never heard of anything so ridiculous. There are no cats in or on the ocean; they don't like water—not even on their paws. This fog is scary because you don't know where you are or where you came from or are going to. At first I thought I had some Kleenex stuck in my eyes from Missus's wiping them, but nobody else could see much either. Missus said, "We will soon be there." But a lady called Gertrude Stein said, "When you get there, there isn't any there there." I couldn't tell where the sea left off and the sky began or where the islands were. Also, things smelled different. Damp. I heard other boats, but I couldn't see them. My ears got blasted off because M kept screeching a horn to warn people we were coming. I don't understand: weren't they coming or going too? My worst thoughts were that I would never be able to find Jazz again, and our love might disappear into the fog.

Some English friends arrived for a visit, which cheered us up. They are used to all this wet, gray stuff and think nothing of it. The accident rate must be very high in England, with cars bashing into one another in the fog; but this does not concern me because I'll never go there. I'm told there is a rule that prevents dogs from other countries from visiting their friends in England, in case they have rabies and would spread it. That's dumb. I've had rabies shots, so I can't get it and never will. I should be allowed to go anywhere. Jazz, too.

These English people are terribly nice, despite their senseless rules. They have dogs and cats of their own, and from the way they treated me, you would think they had come all this long way just to meet ME. And Cat, maybe.

They wanted to eat some lobsters, so M decided to take

them to the Fishermen's Dock to buy some, giving them a boat ride around the islands, too. Missus took advantage of their absence to take a shower, and I decided to see them off in the little boat.

After they left, I got to snuffing around on the float, picking up bird droppings and bits of salty, tasty shellfish. I wasn't looking where I was going, and suddenly I came to the edge of the float and just fell in. I'm not sure how it happened, but that doesn't matter because I am not going to practice doing it again. I just plopped over, and it was as wet and cold as I remembered.

Since the shore was far away, I paddled around the float to find a place where I could climb out. I couldn't use their swimming ladder or find anything else. I got very tired and scared. At last I found a strut underneath the float that I could climb up on, and there I waited.

Meanwhile, Missus had something she called a "gut reaction"—a simple feeling that all was not well and I was in trouble. She looked down the hill to the float, and there I wasn't. She called and called. No answer. She picked up her towel and ran down as fast as she could, with that awful feeling growing into a real panic that I had drowned.

She couldn't find me anywhere and thought that maybe I had gone off in the boat with the English people. Then she heard the jangle of my rabies and I.D. tags when I tried to shake myself. She lay down on the float and peered underneath and saw me, shivering and shaking on the strut. She tried to reach me carefully without falling in but couldn't quite—it was a matter of inches. So she made a lunge, barely getting hold of my collar, and pulled me off the strut and lifted me up on the float. Sun, glorious sun! Missus was near tears as we both ran up the hill. She got another towel and rubbed me almost dry, all the time asking me, "Why didn't you bark? Why didn't you whine or cry to let me know where you were?" I don't know, I don't know. I am not a great barker, I guess. Never have been.

Soon enough we heard M and the English people returning. Little did they realize what drama they had missed! Missus was giggling about it, because it could have been embarrassing if they had come back earlier and found her lying on the float with no clothes on.

They came up the hill to show us the lobsters. Maybe they wondered why we looked so bedraggled, but they asked no questions. The emphasis was definitely on lobsters. I went over to see them and give them a sniff. Nothing to get excited about, I thought. They were wet and cold, just like me. Except they know how to live in the water, and I don't.

M put them in the fridge with an evil grin on his face, as if to say "See you later, lobbies." I don't think they understood. Two hours later they were cooked and eaten. I guess they were good. There was nothing left but the shells. Cat didn't even get any.

End of this saga: some died; I was saved. I guess those English rulers have something for me to be grateful for, after all. Without that extra rabies tag to jangle against the I.D., I might never have been found under the float. Perhaps I'd better practice barking more.

Bones and Bird Seed

Missus gave me a special beef marrow bone to chew on when we were still in Cambridge. Since it was a big one, I hadn't finished gnawing it, so we brought it to the island, where I could chew on it during the boring, nothing-to-do times.

I was working on it slowly one evening before bedtime, and I swallowed the remains of the whole bone by mistake on purpose. But it was bigger than I had thought, and it hurt going down and got stuck inside me. I couldn't cough it up, so I just sat there, drooling.

Missus realized I had stopped gnawing and looked up from her reading. She said, "Where is the bone?" Usually I answer that question by going to fetch it, but this time I just sat and looked at her. It didn't take her long to understand the problem.

Our phone was out of order and the fog was thick. We weren't going to go anywhere in case we got lost so late at night. It was a Sunday, anyway, so the vet's office would be closed. There was nothing for me to do but sit up all night on the bed, leaning on Missus's legs, as it hurt too much to lie down. It was a long night for all of us except Cat, who slept through the whole episode.

At five the next morning we decided to go to town so we could at least telephone the vet. We set off in the little boat after breakfast, despite the fog. It was the dawn of a very long day.

We docked the boat, made a fruitless phone call, as

there was no answer: so decided to drive over to the next town, where the vet lived and had her Office. It was still closed when we got there, but by good luck she looked out the window and saw us parked and let us in immediately. She lifted me carefully and put me down to X-ray. Sure enough, the pictures showed the bone, stuck near my heart and lungs. However, not having the equipment to go down my throat and get it out, she sent us on to the bigger hospital, where another vet might be able to help me.

I was feeling pretty awful, and M and M were already tired and worried; but there was nothing else to do but drive over there and wait to meet him.

The doctor said he would try to do an endoscopy—putting a special pipe down my throat—but he made no promises about the outcome ... or in-go.

He stuck a pin in me, making me drowsy. I don't know what happened, but I heard him tell M and M later that he could not get the bone or even dislodge it. He said there was little hope, so he suggested that we drive back to Boston, to the Angell, or over to Grafton to the Tufts hospital. Both were nearly five hours away.

Then he remembered that a new hospital had opened near Brunswick and Bath where there were some excellent doctors, so he phoned to see if we could go there. Indeed, we were told to come immediately.It was then nearly noon, but M and M didn't want to take the time to stop for lunch, so they picked up some snacks. For once, I didn't want anything to eat.

M was driving so fast down a hill that he got a ticket for speeding: a cop was waiting for him at the bottom. It was just unfair, and if I'd been awake I'd have barked at him and scared him off. M didn't tell him why he was going so fast, which might have canceled the whole thing. This was getting to be an expensive day.

We found the hospital and met the vet, who was kind and hopeful that he could either get the bone out or move it into my stomach. Then he could operate and remove it entirely. He had some tricks the other vet didn't know about. However, he said that if he was unable to do this by endoscopy, I might not survive chest surgery. I wasn't sure what he meant, but Missus's eyes got all blurry.

He stuck me with another pin, and I fell asleep and didn't know what happened. But M and M told me he came out of the operating room a half hour later with the bone in his hand, successfully pulled out of my throat. Everyone in the waiting room cheered and clapped, and Missus was so overwhelmed, she jumped up and gave him a big hug. He was pleased, too, and said it had been a very "rewarding experience."

So we started off again, hoping to make it back home before dark. Three hours later we were back in the harbor and in our boat. The sun was setting and the fog was coming in fast, but we made it back to the island, moored the boat, and climbed the hill to the house by nine o'clock. I was wobbly on my legs and kept bumping into the furniture, which made M and M laugh. Missus gave me some mushy stuff for supper and some water.

I was so glad to be home and able to lie down again in comfort. We'd been gone for almost fifteen hours, seen three vets, and driven many miles. Sleeping was good.

What really amazed Missus was that, after the news got around town, someone stopped her on the street and said, "You mean to say you drove all that distance just for a DOG?" I don't think Missus answered her. But a real friend sent me a box of wonderful biscuits as a get-well present.

When my throat was better, I got very hungry again but was told NO MORE BONES. However, I found something else that was quite delicious to pass the time of day.

Last summer M wanted to attract some birds to our porch, so he bought a big bag of bird seed. The birds didn't know this, so they never showed up. Maybe Cat and I scared them off. Anyway, he hung the bag on a hook in the shed for the winter. Either the bag broke or a chippy poked a hole in it—but no matter, the result was absolutely fabulous. A pound or more of seed fell on the floor of the shed, and there it was, tasting like chopped nuts, just waiting to be eaten. So I did.

M and M were calling me to go for a walk, but of course I was too busy to come. Missus came looking and found me in the shed, cleaning up the mess so she wouldn't have to. Very thoughtful.

She waited to see if I was going to throw up and be sick, but nothing happened. But when we went walking the next day, things came out all seeds and more seeds. This lasted for three days.

By then Missus had cleaned up what was left of the bird seed, so I never got a second chance. Now I am back to my old, dull dog food. Not very exciting, but more healthy, I suppose.

Smelly Days

A lot of people who don't live on an island ask us what we do all day. They must think that living on an island means total isolation and boredom. Ridiculous. Missus tells them that we do all the things they do on the mainland except drive cars. We go everywhere by boat, which is a wonderful change from the winter, when we have to use cars all the time. We love our expeditions, short ones for errands, medium ones for picnics, or long ones for weekends. But the other day was not so pleasant, and we wished we had been in a car to get away quickly. We got stuck in a bunch of dead fish.

Some friends wanted to join us in the late afternoon for a trip around the islands to watch the sun set and the moon rise. I was invited, too, because I am good at cleaning up all the chips, nuts, and crumbs.

As we were going along, we saw a mass of white things floating on the surface, and before we knew it, we were in the middle of a stinking mess. Fish were floating belly up by the thousands. We passed a small sailboat, and since the wind had gone down with the sun, there were no breezes to push it along quickly. But we went along as fast as possible to get clear of the dead fish; the stench was suffocating.

What we didn't expect to see, or smell, when we got home were the masses of the dead Pogies on our beach. The ebbing tide had left a mess of them stranded on the rocks, and it was still going out and leaving more.

No one wanted fish for supper that night. I got my usual meal, and M and M and our friends had lamb chops. The house stunk, and we lost our appetites. We spent a very smelly night, even with closed windows. Our friends decided suddenly that they had to leave the next morning. It seems they had forgotten some very important engagement. I suppose, when "the going gets smelly, ..." M and M took them to town after breakfast. When they came back, they got some big boxes and went to the beach to rake up the dead fish that the returning tide had still left for us. Missus put a scarf over her nose to absorb the odor. I thought I'd try eating a fish after I'd rolled on it. After all, M and M spend money to buy dead fish, so why not give it a try? It really wasn't any good, though I did roll on it once more. I didn't realize that my action would lead to a bath.

M and M put all the boxes they could fit into the little boat and went out, far away to the big ocean to dump them, hoping they wouldn't wash back in again. When they came back, the hosed out the boat and took showers, but essence of Pogie still lingered. It was there two days later, even though the tide had come and gone many times. Finally it rained and things got better.

My sensitive nose was breathing good air once again when something terrible happened to it. A big, gray, baglike thing was hanging down from a low branch of a tree; a humming sound was coming from it and I wanted to investigate. I found out. Lots of small buzz-hums came out and stuck pins into my nose. They hurt. I ran inside to Missus and just lay down beside her.

She didn't notice anything wrong right away, but I was feeling awful. Then her grandson said, "Bunter stuck his nose in a wasps' nest." She knelt down immediately and saw that my nose was all swollen. Then she phoned the vet, who told her to give me some pills, which, luckily, she already had in the house. She also put cortisone ointment on my bites. That helped some, and later I felt a little better. But my nose was lopsided for a long time. I certainly learned about bugs that sting.

F_{inal} D_{ays}

. . .

Autumn Days, Cooler Days

It is getting colder up here in Maine, now that fall has come. M and M are getting ready to drive home for the winter. I am used to the routine after so many summers on the island, and I don't like it. The only good thing is that I get some leftovers from the fridge, which has to be emptied. We have to close up doors and windows, fuss about locks, beds, laundry, and put away all my old toys.

I have a strange feeling that I may not be back next year. My tummy hurts a lot now. I don't know what it is or why, and I wish the pain would go away. Missus looks at me with loving questions in her eyes.

M lights fires every morning to take the chill off, which is comforting, because I don't have the energy to run about and get warm. Cat sleeps most of the time also. Missus gave her extra blankets to curl up in, since she is very thin. She also put a hot water bottle under her blanket when the temperature was only forty-five degrees. Unfortunately, Missus didn't check it for leaks, and it dribbled all night. Cat got quite wet, and the sofa was drenched. Missus thought it was Cat's fault,

but when she picked up the bottle and saw it was leaking, she didn't blame Cat at all.

Cat doesn't like water. Never did. Neither do I much. Of course I swim because I've had to, after falling in; and I've learned to tolerate baths because I've had to. But Cat has never had to swim, and I don't think she has ever had a real bath. I heard that she had fallen in the tub once when she was a kitten. She was trying to walk around the edge of it and lost her balance. I wish I'd been there! Missus took her right out, but she was very upset and hasn't been near a bath since.

Cat knows all about packing up to leave. The minute she sees her travel box and the suitcases come out, she decides to go out hunting and not return for a long, long time. She knows that M and M wouldn't leave without her. But they also have a time schedule for returning home, so they can't delay for days and days. After observing Cat for many years, Missus has learned to lure Cat upstairs to a certain room, where there is some delicious food: then she closes the door tight before she gets out the travel box and suitcases. One time, however, Cat smelled a big, fat rat and dashed out the back door when she saw Missus coming to get her. She didn't show up for hours and hours, and it got too late to leave that day. It was then that I knew who ran the household.

Later

I kept wondering if the long trip home in September was my last one. Missus took me to my vet soon after we returned. He said I was getting old and was very sick. I didn't like this. If this is part of aging, I don't want it. No, not at all. It seems to have a lot to do with Time, which I don't understand either. M and M are always complaining that there isn't enough of it. M says he will be back in two minutes. It's more like two hours. Missus says she will be back soon. When is soon? They say, "Wait a minute, and I'll tell you." Well, I wait, but with no results. Sometimes I think I've spent my whole life just waiting. I heard a good definition of Time recently, at least one I can sort of understand: "Time is something that happens, to prevent everything else from happening all at once." There is no way I could eat all my suppers, sleep all my sleeps, and do everything all in one second. So I'd better think differently about Time, and enjoy it as it passes. But it did get me thinking about when I was born and for what purpose—noble or ig-.

A certain lady walks her dog every day past our driveway. She said she would invite me to her dog's birthday party, but she never did—or at least I didn't get the invitation. Then I realized that I had never had a party just for ME— with beef bones, biscuits, and other dogs to play with.

I think I am seventy-something now, in dog years, and that is a LOT of parties. If M and M were dogs, they would be over 490 years old by now. (Sometimes they act it.) They certainly are "chronologically gifted": Cat is nine- teen and according to dog/cat age she is 133. (She acts it, too.) I think it is better to stay young. Anyway, no matter how you play these numbers, I will always be younger than

Cat, even though my chin and ears are lined with white fur now, and this time it isn't paint. I need some black powder to cover them up. Missus puts powder on her face every day, though I can't see that it makes much difference. She looks into a piece of glass and says, "Well, that's not half bad." That word half is an odd one, too. It either is

enough or isn't. When I've eaten half my supper and my bowl is half empty, it isn't half enough for me! And I remember, when I was younger, I tried to jump off our boat to the float, when we were landing. I took a wild leap and only made it halfway—into that freezing water. Missus tells me that I remember only half of the commands I learned as a puppy, but I don't know which half. Well, it doesn't matter now. I have a feeling that I have a lot less than half my life to live.

Not Good Times

I've just had my 3,644th walk. Well, since arithmetic is not my strong point, I may be off by a few hundred one way or another. I've been taking M or Missus for walks ever since I came to live with them ten years ago—perhaps twice a day, perhaps not at all, depending on the weather. But it has been a lot of padding around in general, no matter how you look at it, and more so for me than for them, since they only take one step to my four.

My tummy is all swollen now, and I have a hard time getting comfortable, either lying down or just sitting. Climbing the stairs is worse, so Missus sometimes carries me up to bed. I've been taking my pills for so long I've lost track, but they aren't doing me any good. I don't "seize up" anymore, but the vet says I have a liver problem. He calls it a "trade-off. I think he is saying that, though the pills may have stopped my seizures, they have also ruined my liver.

M asks if I want to play ball. I don't really, but I want to please him. It makes M and M feel better if I can do things with them, because they don't know exactly what else to do except wait and hope I'll get better.

No, that isn't going to happen. I think I know something that they don't know—or won't accept. I sit and stare hard at Missus for help. She and M hold me close, and that is comforting. I've loved my life with them—the games we've played, the food I've eaten, the walks, the drives, the trips we've had together. Who will be with them if I'm not here?

I can't find Cat anywhere. She was getting very thin and didn't move about much, but she went to sleep on M and M's bed a few days ago. Missus spent some time caressing her and talking to her, but she didn't respond much. I wonder if she was feeling as awful as I do. A vet came to the house and went upstairs to see her, and after that she disappeared. I hope she is happy wherever she is. I miss her very much. I didn't realize what a big part of my life she was, my full-time four-legged companion.

I wonder where I am going, and if I will disappear too? Whatever happens, I hope I won't hurt anymore. I look deeply into Missus's eyes, asking for more help. M and M hold me and love me and that is soothing and reassuring. But I am very tired right now, and think I will go and sleep for a while.

Epilogue

In February, Bunter was given a lethal injection to release him from his misery. M and M stayed went with him, and Missus held him in her arms while he slipped away.

People asked why we put ourselves through such anguish. We owed it to Bunter because of the ten-year gift he had given us, of trust, love, and joy. How could we do less? A dog is for life.

There were phone calls, letters, and a poem from friends who had known and loved him. Two trees were planted in his memory by a close friend. Bunter will always be a part of their lives. His collar is intertwined with Cat's in her garden grave.